LITTLE QUICK FIX:

SELECT A SAMPLE

Sara Miller McCune founded SAGE Publishing in 1965 to support the dissemination of usable knowledge and educate a global community. SAGE publishes more than 1000 journals and over 800 new books each year, spanning a wide range of subject areas. Our growing selection of library products includes archives, data, case studies and video. SAGE remains majority owned by our founder and after her lifetime will become owned by a charitable trust that secures the company's continued independence.

Los Angeles | London | New Delhi | Singapore | Washington DC | Melbourne

LITTLE QUICK FIX:

SELECT A SAMPLE

Paul
Silvia

Los Angeles | London | New Delhi
Singapore | Washington DC | Melbourne

Los Angeles | London | New Delhi
Singapore | Washington DC | Melbourne

SAGE Publications Ltd
1 Oliver's Yard
55 City Road
London EC1Y 1SP

SAGE Publications Inc.
2455 Teller Road
Thousand Oaks, California 91320

SAGE Publications India Pvt Ltd
B 1/I 1 Mohan Cooperative Industrial Area
Mathura Road
New Delhi 110 044

SAGE Publications Asia-Pacific Pte Ltd
3 Church Street
#10-04 Samsung Hub
Singapore 049483

Editor: Alysha Owen
Editorial assistant: Lauren Jacobs
Production editor: Victoria Nicholas
Marketing manager: Ben Griffin-Sherwood
Cover design: Shaun Mercier
Typeset by: C&M Digitals (P) Ltd, Chennai, India
Printed in the UK

Library of Congress Control Number: 2019949963

British Library Cataloguing in Publication data

A catalogue record for this book is available
from the British Library

ISBN 978-1-5297-0899-8

At SAGE we take sustainability seriously. Most of our products are printed in the UK using responsibly
sourced papers and boards. When we print overseas we ensure sustainable papers are used as measured
by the PREPS grading system. We undertake an annual audit to monitor our sustainability.

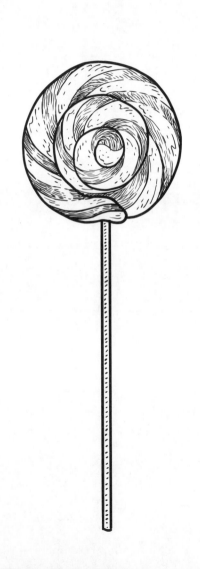

Contents

2 MIN summary

Everything in this book!

Section 1   Sampling is studying a 'part' to understand the 'whole'. Studying samples enables researchers to understand large, dispersed groups.

Section 2   Your population is the broader group you want to understand, not 'everyone everywhere'. Defining your population narrowly gives your project focus and credibility.

Section 3   Probability sampling methods, the gold standard in sampling, should be your first choice. They create a small-scale replica of the population by randomly selecting members from it.

Section 4   Because non-probability methods – quota, convenience, and purposive sampling – introduce subjective judgment into the sampling process, you should view them as fallbacks for when probability sampling isn't feasible.

Section 5 Asking participants for referrals, known as snowball sampling, lets you recruit members of ill-defined, hard-to-reach, and wary populations.

Section 6 To sample ethically, researchers must think through the legal and ethical issues and consult their local ethics office.

Section 7 Reducing error involves targeting both random error and systematic, consistent biases in sampling.

Section 8 Plan for the largest feasible sample size: large samples reduce your margin of error and increase statistical power.

Section

1

Studying samples
enables researchers
to understand large,
dispersed groups

What is sampling?

10 SEC summary

Sampling is selecting and
studying 'some' to draw
conclusions about 'all'.

Who do you want to study?

Instead of studying a whole population, researchers study a sample – a smaller group – because most populations are too large, far-flung, and hard to reach. Sampling a subset of the population is an efficient alternative that balances research quality (the validity and credibility of your conclusions) with feasibility.

Researchers can sample anything – objects, institutions, and countries, to name a few – but sampling people raises unique practical and legal issues. Because people are so diverse, no human population is easily captured by a handful of people. And because we can't force people to participate in research, ethical and legal obligations constrain our sampling plans. The craft of real-world sampling involves balancing research quality, resources, and ethics.

PARTS AND WHOLES

Sampling is selecting 'some' to make inferences about 'all', selecting parts to draw conclusions about the whole. You create a sample by selecting elements from a population.

- Your population is the 'all' that you want to understand. In a study of voter apathy, for example, the population might be all eligible voters in New Zealand.

- Your elements – also known as units or members – are the parts you select from the whole. In our example, the population (eligible voters in New Zealand) has around 3,700,000 elements (individual people).

- Your sample is the resulting group of elements. A group of 2,000 eligible voters who completed the survey, for example, would be our sample of the population of Kiwi voters.

WHY DO RESEARCHERS SELECT SAMPLES?

Researchers study samples because of ever-pesky reality. Most human populations that interest social scientists are large, dispersed, and not easily reached. Surveying the population of 3,700,000 New Zealand voters, for example, would be extraordinarily expensive.

By sampling part of the population, researchers balance research quality and feasibility. Quality projects make claims that are *valid* (likely to be true) and *credible* (likely to persuade the project's audience). Feasible projects have the necessary resources – money, personnel, and time – to execute the project.

YOU CAN SAMPLE ANYTHING

Researchers in the social and behavioral sciences commonly sample people to learn about human populations, but the logic of sampling applies to all kinds of populations. Your work might involve sampling elements like artifacts, institutions, epochs, or environments.

Sampling is important for non-scholarly purposes too. A quality-control manager in a shampoo factory will test only a few bottles to appraise the day's output; an apple farmer will sample only a handful of apples to evaluate the ripeness of the orchard. As in scholarly sampling, these sampling decisions reflect realistic constraints – you can't bite into every apple and still have a crop.

SAMPLING PEOPLE IS PECULIARLY VEXING

Although the theory doesn't change, sampling people is uniquely complicated. First, people are diverse. Unlike apples and shampoo bottles, humans are incredibly varied. Because we almost always expect a population of people to be diverse and complex, no population is credibly represented by a handful of people.

Second, ethical and legal obligations constrain sampling. Our apple farmer can yank any apple she wants from her trees, but researchers can't force people to take part in research. Identifying and contacting people for research can potentially put them at risk.

SETTING THE STAGE FOR SAMPLING

Let's do some early brainstorming about your project – we'll refine these rough ideas later.

Ask yourself:

1   How diverse is the population you expect to study?

Think about common demographic factors – age, gender, employment, relationship status, and social class, to name a few. How varied are your population members?

2   What ethical and legal issues stand out?

Do you expect to contact anyone who might be unable to give consent?

• Some people can't legally consent, such as children or people under guardianship.

• Other people might not understand what you're asking, such as those who have limited comprehension of your language.

Do you have a plan for data privacy and security?

- Do you really need to collect identifying data, like names, contact information, and likenesses?

- If you do, how will you keep the research records and data secure and private? Where will you keep digital and paper records? Who else will have access?

3   What resources are available?

How much money might the project cost?

- Think about everything from copies, travel, incentives, and research help.

Who can help?

- Will anyone, from supervisors to fellow students, help you collect or analyse the data? What will help cost you in money or favours owed?

How much time do you have to finish the project?

- Do you have a 'hard deadline' driven by a degree requirement? Working backward, how many months do you have?

Defining your population
narrowly gives your project
focus and credibility

2

Section

What is my population?

10 SEC summary

The larger group of people you would like to make valid, credible claims about – not everyone everywhere.

summary

We study samples to learn about populations

Populations are where the intellectual action is. Samples are rarely important in their own right; instead, they are a means to the end of understanding larger groups. Defining your population is sampling's starting point. Students often think about populations too expansively, like 'everyone in my country'. Researchers, in contrast, view populations more narrowly and practically: your population is the group that you want to understand.

Institutions and governments commonly study entire populations via censuses, and some fields study populations directly. But in most cases, researchers can study only a sample, so they must select one that illuminates their population of interest.

WHAT YOUR POPULATION ISN'T

You can't sample without first defining your population. To sharpen your definition, let's look at what your project's population probably isn't:

- Distant people from divergent cultures on the other side of the world.
- Everyone currently alive.
- The 'general population' of people currently residing in your country.

Researchers think about populations in ways that are focused and pragmatic.

- When planning your project, your population is who you want to understand.
- After collecting data, your population is who you can make valid, credible claims about.

Focused claims about narrow, defined populations, such as 'first-year teachers in urban Canadian school districts', are more credible than claims about vague ones, such as 'new teachers'.

GENERALIZING FROM SAMPLES TO POPULATIONS

Viewing populations as 'the group researchers want to understand' helps us think about generalizing from samples to populations. First, we should judge a sample's quality and generalizability based on its intended population, not on some other population that we wish the researchers had targeted instead.

Second, generalizing isn't a binary, all-or-none issue. Projects have levels of 'population-ness', ranging from a core group to increasingly distal groups. Your research can shed light on many groups, but your claims become more uncertain as you move outward from the core.

DEFINING YOUR POPULATION

Defining your population is like peeling away layers of an onion, but with fewer tears.

Thinking about your own research, jot down your thoughts below.

1   First define your population's **core** – it's the group that comes up when you complete statements like 'The group I most want to understand is ...'

....

....

....

2   Next comes your **inner layer**, the groups that resemble your core population. These groups appear when you say 'Although my project doesn't specifically study them, its findings should be useful for researchers who study ...'

....

....

....

3   For your population's **outer layer**, you have distal groups that
    share some features but are obviously distinct. You'll find them
    at the end of phrases like 'Although they aren't the focus of my
    project, my findings might shed some light on …'

....

....

....

4   Finally, the groups **outside your population** appear in statements
    like 'I don't expect my work to be relevant to …'

....

....

....

WHY DON'T I JUST STUDY THE WHOLE POPULATION?

Governments and institutions routinely study populations via a census – a survey of an entire population. A census can cover populations large and small, from a census of all residents of Portugal to a census of all 120 first-year students at a small college. And some researchers do too. This is the province of demography and population science, the study of whole populations.

DO I ALWAYS HAVE A BROADER POPULATION?

Usually, yes. Scholarship seeks to make general claims – to go beyond the time, place, and sample of a single research project. Samples usually aren't interesting per se. They're valuable because they illuminate the population that we're interested in.

But sometimes you don't have a population. Your project might be a small-scale census, like all first-year teachers in a school. Or your project might be a programme evaluation, which appraises how well a programme worked in a specific setting.

Ultimately, your project's 'population-ness' depends on the claims you want to make. If you want to draw inferences about a larger group – first-year teachers in other schools, or how the program might fare elsewhere – then you have a population.

WHAT IF I ALREADY HAVE A SAMPLE?

You already have a sample if your project uses existing data. Some studies are so intricate, vast, and expensive that institutions and governments conduct them and archive the data for scholars to use. It's wise to use these impressive studies, with their top-notch sampling designs, instead of reinventing a smaller, shabbier wheel.

But existing datasets have two caveats:

1   You inherit the original study's flaws, so you must still
    understand its sampling design to know what claims you can make
    about the population.

2   Samples go stale when populations evolve away from a dataset's
    original population. Samples of married couples collected when
    only heterosexual marriage was legal, for example, misrepresent
    the modern population of married couples.

Get it?

Q: If you asked a researcher to explain what a population is, what would be a good answer?

Got it!

A: A population is a group that we want to understand and make claims about.

#LittleQuickFix

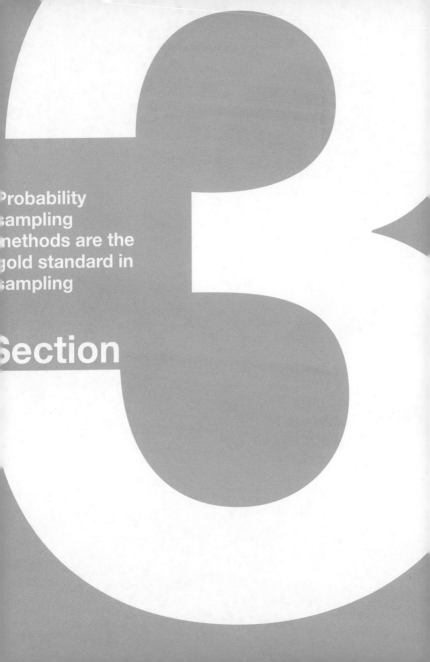

Probability
sampling
methods are the
gold standard in
sampling

Section

Should I use probability sampling?

A

summary

Yes, whenever possible – it is the
gold standard for sampling. When
done well, it creates a small-scale
model of your population.

summary

Your population in miniature

Probability sampling creates a sample that is a miniature model of the population. When you use probability sampling, your sample is like a tiny table in a doll's house – it matches the real thing in all the ways that matter, only smaller. Because the model is like the population, only smaller, we can make valid, credible claims about populations from probability samples.

But there's no free lunch in research. Probability sampling is superior, but it's also more intricate and often impractical. Even when a population is well defined, you may be unable, for ethical or practical reasons, to identify and contact its members.

WHAT IS PROBABILITY SAMPLING?

In probability sampling, you select a sample that mirrors the population by applying basic probability theory. A probability sample has two features:

- Every population member has a non-zero chance of being selected for your sample – no one is definitely excluded (a chance of zero).

- You know what this probability of selection is.

For example, imagine researchers at a large university with 4,000 undergraduate psychology majors. They would like to select a sample of 400 majors to survey about their career goals. Using probability sampling, the researchers would follow four steps:

1   Define the population.

2   Develop a sampling frame – a 'list' of population members.

3   Select a sample using probability methods.

4   Contact the selected members.

THE SAMPLING FRAME IS THE LINCHPIN

Probability sampling requires a sampling frame: a comprehensive, well-defined list of the population to draw from. For the practical purposes of your project, the sampling frame defines your population.

In our example, the university can provide a list of students who fit the population definition ('currently enrolled undergraduate students with psychology as a major'). That list is the sampling frame.

Poor sampling frames cause error and bias. When you obtain or make a list, check it twice: Does your list include everyone it ought to include? Does it systematically miss some members?

BRAINSTORMING FRAMES

For your population, what is your sampling frame?

- Is there a ready-made list that you can access, such as a list of attendees at an education conference or a list of students awarded degrees?

- Is there a database you can access? Many organizations and professional societies will lend or sell lists of contact information.

- Can you create a list from public records, such as all couples who applied for a marriage license in the past year? Are there public directories you can mine, like the contact information for all school administrators in your district?

SELECTING
YOUR SAMPLE

Once you have your list of the population, you select elements to create
your sample.

Random sampling, the simplest method, randomly selects elements
from the sampling frame. From the frame of 4,000 students, we would
randomly select 400. With simple random sampling, each person in
the sampling frame has the same known, non-zero chance of being
included: 400/4000, or 10%.

Stratified random sampling is a useful extension for when you want to ensure that your sample matches some feature of the population. In our example, imagine that 75% of the psychology-student population identifies as female and 25% identifies as male. With simple random sampling, the fickle nature of randomness means that the sample won't always be exactly 75% female. It should be close most of the time, but it will occasionally be way off.

To prevent this, we first split our sampling frame into groups, known as strata: a female group (3,000 people) and a male group (1,000 people). Using simple random sampling within each strata, we then select 300 women and 100 men. Stratified random sampling guarantees that our sample will match the population on the stratified variable.

PROS AND CONS OF PROBABILITY SAMPLING

Probability sampling, when done well, provides a miniature replica of your population, so you can draw conclusions about the population that are valid and credible. Researchers should use this family of tools whenever possible. These sampling designs are hallmarks of high-quality, large-scale surveys.

The catch, however, is that probability sampling isn't always practical or possible. Privacy concerns and data-protection laws have made it much harder to obtain comprehensive sampling frames, and probability sampling is impossible when the population is obscure.

Non-probability methods

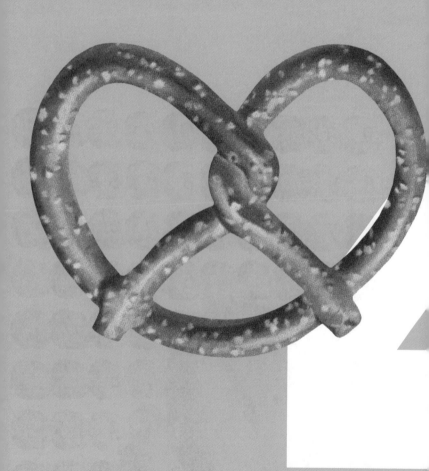

Section

4

Should I use subjective, non-probability sampling?

summary

You should consider subjective sampling methods when probability sampling isn't practical or possible.

Lighting a candle versus cursing the darkness

Probability sampling is superior, but in sampling, as in life, we can't always have the best. Non-probability sampling – sometimes called subjective sampling – has an important place in research. In common **subjective sampling** methods, a member's chance of being selected for a sample can be unknown or predetermined.

Researchers shouldn't let perfect be the enemy of the good – subjective sampling can shed light on problems when probability sampling isn't feasible. But even when these methods are the only option, researchers must still think through the implications of non-probability sampling for the validity and credibility of the conclusions they would like to draw.

The alternative to probability sampling, in the literal lingo of sampling theory, is non-probability sampling. Non-probability samples rely on the subjective judgments of researchers, so these methods are often called subjective sampling. They will not yield a sample that is your population in miniature.

Non-probability samples have these features:

- The researcher doesn't know each member's probability of being selected.

- The sample will never be a random subset of the population because some elements are usually guaranteed to be omitted (a chance of zero) or to be included (a chance of 1).

Because a person's chance of selection can be unknown or pre-determined, sampling is not driven simply by probability.

NON-
PROBABILITY
SAMPLING

Why would researchers use subjective sampling when it's worse?

1   Some populations are poorly understood and hard to define.

2   There may be no ethical or practical way to develop a sampling
     frame.

3   Many research projects have tight timelines and budgets.

4   Subjective sampling is efficient for small-scale pilot and proof-of-
     concept studies.

Quota sampling sets sample-size targets ('quotas') for different categories and recruits until the quotas are filled. For our example survey of psychology majors, researchers would set quotas of 300 women and 100 men. Once a quota is met, researchers stop collecting data for that category and keep collecting in the others.

Although quota sampling superficially looks like stratified random sampling, it is different and worse. Unlike probability sampling, quota sampling isn't wholly random: if someone turns you down, you keep going until you fill your sample size quota. As a result, some population members have no chance of being selected. Once the quota of 300 women is filled, for example, all remaining women in the population have zero chance of being selected.

QUOTA
SAMPLING

Quota sampling guarantees desired sample sizes in each category, but a quota sample usually consists of the population members who were easy to find and willing to take part. These members may differ from the population in important ways. Serious bias can happen when one quota group – women or men, conservative or liberal, old or young – is more accessible and willing than another. This flaw has caused some spectacular failures in the history of political polling.

Although the label convenience sampling is a common synonym for non-probability sampling, it's actually a specific kind. Convenience sampling has two flavours: 'at hand' and 'opt in'.

In at-hand sampling, researchers select participants because they're easy to identify and contact, like conducting surveys in a busy public place. In opt-in sampling, researchers publicize the study – such as with flyers, print ads, email blasts, and social-media posts – and participants 'opt in' to doing it by contacting the researchers. In at-hand sampling, researchers decide which participants to contact; in opt-in sampling, participants decide which study to select, if any.

Convenience sampling is never ideal, but it is always feasible when resources are low. Opt-in sampling is often the only way to study narrow groups for which there's no sampling frame, such as parents of binational children or adults with major depression. Nevertheless, the fact that all participants have self-selected into the study can cause complex sampling biases.

CONVENIENCE SAMPLING

Purposive sampling picks some or all units based on expert judgment. Depending on the project, you might pick elements that are atypical, common, or both. This design often involves randomly selecting many elements but purposively selecting others.

Purposive sampling is common when an audience expects some elements to be included. For a study of early-career teachers, for example, an audience of administrators might expect to see the winners of teaching awards included. If you're selecting countries for a study of economic inequality, your committee will surely want to see your own country included and probably expect to see the most and least equal ones as well. Purposive sampling can thus increase a project's credibility.

PURPOSIVE SAMPLING

Have a go at matching each sampling method with its design

1   A researcher who wants to recruit young children for a study of cognitive development posts flyers about her project at local day-cares, pediatrics offices, and community centers.

Sampling method: ....

2   For a study comparing 40 first-year teachers to 40 senior teachers, a researcher mails paper surveys. Because he got 40 completed first-year surveys first, he stopped recruiting those teachers and focused his recruiting efforts on the senior teachers.

Sampling method: ....

3   For a study of job burnout among hospital nurses, a researcher used random sampling from a sampling frame acquired from a hospital network to obtain a sample of 140 nurses. To enrich the probability sample, she recruited an additional 20 nurses from a hospital known for being understaffed and strained.

Sampling method: ....

4   A researcher interested in LGBTQ members of conservative
     political parties gains permission to post a weblink to his survey on
     several social media groups popular among that population.

Sampling method: ....

5   A researcher wants to interview 20 trainee teachers. To ensure
     that some high-performing trainees appear in the sample, she
     asks school administrators to identify both talented and average
     trainees for her to contact.

Sampling method: ....

6   Researchers designing a study of well-being among new mothers
     want to recruit 200 women: 100 who are legally married and 100
     who are not. They plan to keep contacting potential participants in
     each group until they reach 100.

Sampling method: ....

7   To assess how much stress university students experience
     about their finances, the researchers fan out across campus with
     clipboards and ask students passing by to complete a short,
     anonymous survey.

Sampling method: ....

Check your answers

1   Convenience sampling

2   Quota sampling

3   Purposive sampling

4   Convenience sampling

5   Purposive sampling

6   Quota sampling

7   Convenience sampling

JUSTIFY YOUR METHOD

DO IT YOURSELF

Could your project feasibly use probability sampling?

YES/NO

If NO, what kind of non-probability sampling will you use?

☐ QUOTA

☐ CONVENIENCE: At hand

☐ CONVENIENCE: Opt in

☐ PURPOSIVE

How would you explain your sampling design to a thesis committee?

If you are not using probability sampling, what are your reasons for this?

....

....

What are the likely limitations and biases of your design?

....

....

Section

5

Snowball sampling

How do I sample from ill-defined, hard-to-reach, and wary populations?

summary

By asking early participants for referrals, you can access populations that are hard to sample.

Thorny Populations

Some populations are harder to sample. We don't know enough about some populations – ill-defined ones – to create a sampling frame and identify members. Other populations have members who are hard to reach, so the usual methods for contacting them are ineffective. And in some cases, populations are wary of your project or of science more broadly, so they're reluctant to be found and contacted.

Snowball sampling involves asking participants to refer other potential participants for you to contact. In some cases, participants spread the word directly by contacting other members, thus vouching for the project's legitimacy. A snowball sample can't mirror a population like a probability sample can, but sometimes it's the only option for studying obscure and reluctant groups.

CHALLENGING POPULATIONS

Some kinds of populations bedevil researchers. Many populations are ill-defined and poorly understood, so we don't know their size, boundaries, or composition. Although we have a good sense, for example, of how many legal adults and how many women live in Australia, we don't know how many Australians identify as 'non-aged' or 'non-gendered', and it isn't obvious how we would form a sampling frame for such populations.

Other populations are hard to reach. Often, the whole population is hard to contact, such as people who sell illicit drugs or members of elite social groups. More often, a large subset is vexingly hard to reach. These days, many people will simply ignore your calls, letters, knocks, and emails.

Finally, wary populations are suspicious of you personally or research generally. In some cases, the group's fraught historical relationship with science – eugenics with colonial-era groups, for example – shapes its suspicions.

Think about whether the following features apply to your group. Is your population...

☐ specially concerned with privacy?

☐ transient and moving from place to place, such as people who are homeless?

☐ concerned about violence, such as members of stigmatized and oppressed groups?

☐ sheltered by a layer of 'people' – employees, parents, or guardians – who screen out contact requests?

☐ involved in activity that creates legal risks, such as people who sell illicit drugs and weapons?

☐ skeptical of scholarship or hostile toward your institution?

☐ extremely busy and unlikely to respond to letters and emails from strangers?

☐ defined by a stigmatized activity, such as membership of controversial social groups?

☐ lacking common contact points like permanent mailing addresses, email accounts, and phone numbers?

SNOWBALL SAMPLING

To collect samples of ill-defined, hard-to-reach, and wary populations, researchers often turn to snowball sampling. In most forms of sampling, researchers identify and contact population members; in snowball sampling, population members identify each other.

In a study of the population of sex workers, for example, researchers would first find a few members willing to participate. Those participants are asked for referrals of other sex workers they know. That second wave of participants is then contacted and asked for referrals, and so on. Eventually, the sample size grows like a snowball rolling downhill.

Snowball sampling can be combined with other sampling methods. It's common, for example, to attract an opt-in convenience sample and then ask the opt-in respondents to refer other potential participants.

THE POWER OF VOUCHING

Participants in a snowball sample are sometimes asked to contact other members and publicize the project. With especially hard-to-contact and suspicious populations, researchers may give participants materials – business cards, flyers, or pamphlets – to share with potential sample members.

When current participants identify and contact potential ones, they are vouching for the research project. People who would be wary of you will trust their friend's claim that the study was legitimate, safe, and worthwhile. Snowball sampling is thus a powerful tool for studying reluctant and suspicious populations.

PROS AND CONS

The main strength of snowball sampling is that it allows access to populations that would otherwise be closed off. It is widely used for groups defined by deviant behaviour and for groups that are wary of outsiders.

An obvious limitation is that a snowball sample will never mirror the population like a random probability sample can. But researchers can accept this flaw when the population isn't well-defined or accessible.

A subtle limitation is that snowball samples tend to end up with the population's more popular and connected members. The fringes of the social network – isolated members with few social bonds – are less likely to be referred and sampled.

Section

6

Think through the
legal and ethical
issues

How can
I sample
people
ethically?

summary

When first planning your project,
think about ethical pitfalls and
seek guidance from your local
research ethics committee.

summary

The Ethics of Sampling

Sampling, like all phases of research, requires that thoughtful attention be paid to research ethics. Most of sampling's ethical potholes involve issues of identifying people as members of a population and contacting people to recruit them as participants.

Because social science research often studies populations defined by deviant or controversial features, merely being publicly identified as a member can be harmful or stigmatizing to research participants. Contacting members in ways that respect privacy and autonomy requires thoughtful planning. Legal and ethical frameworks vary across nations and evolve over time, so you should seek guidance from your local research ethics committee when planning your project.

ETHICAL SAMPLING IS FUNDAMENTAL

The history of science is littered with ethical disasters. Ethically flawed research causes layers of harm: to the project's participants, to the society at large, and to the mission of inquiry.

Like all phases of research, sampling entails important ethical issues, especially when sampling people. Most of the potential pitfalls involve identifying people and contacting people. Nations have different relevant laws – especially about privacy, data security, and consent – and diverse ethical frameworks. You should consult your local research ethics committee for up-to-date guidance when planning your project.

AN ETHICS TUNE-UP

DO IT YOURSELF

Go to the webpage of your institution's research ethics committee and look for three things:

1   Data security policies

Where are you allowed – and forbidden – to store physical data, like paper and tapes? What about digital data?

....

....

2   Informed consent

Are you required to obtain informed consent? If so, what are the required elements in a consent form?

....

....

3   Training

Are there upcoming research ethics workshops you can take? What about online modules?

....

....

IDENTIFYING
PEOPLE

For probability sampling, you'll start with a sampling frame – the list that defines your population. For non-probability sampling, you'll end up with a list of people who comprised your sample. You are responsible for the security of these research files.

In some cases, merely being identified publicly as a member of a population – recovering alcoholics, undocumented immigrants, people living out of their cars, women who have had an abortion, families with high net-worth – can create risks and potential harm. Many people, from hackers to law enforcement, would want to see a list of participants defined by illegal or controversial features.

CONTACTING PEOPLE

Contacting members of your population can be illegal, unethical, or unwise. In some cases, the entire population is covered. For example, approaching children to recruit them for research without first seeking their guardians' consent is often forbidden. Many populations have members with a diminished capacity for consent. Limited comprehension of the researcher's language is a common reason; cognitive impairments and medical conditions are others.

Some methods of contacting people will expose their population membership. Consider researchers seeking a sample of people who had recently filed for bankruptcy. Although those court records may be public, sending a postcard invitation to participate exposes the issue to people's roommates, partners, and postal carriers.

For this reason, **opt-in convenience sampling** has some ethical appeal. By allowing population members to choose whether to contact the researchers, it sidesteps many ethical potholes.

COERCION AND INCENTIVES

Informed consent is a cornerstone of research ethics, and researchers obviously cannot coerce people to participate. But for some populations, coercion and consent fall into grey areas. Members of the armed forces, for example, can be ordered to participate in research in some contexts.

Unusually strong incentives are a subtle form of coercion. Financially stressed people, for example, may decide that they can't afford to pass up a large cash incentive despite not wanting to be in your study. Prisoners may feel coerced when participation is rewarded by shaving time off their sentence.

ARE YOU
BEING ETHICAL?

CHECKPOINT

Virtually all institutions have an office or committee that evaluates the
legal and ethical aspects of research.

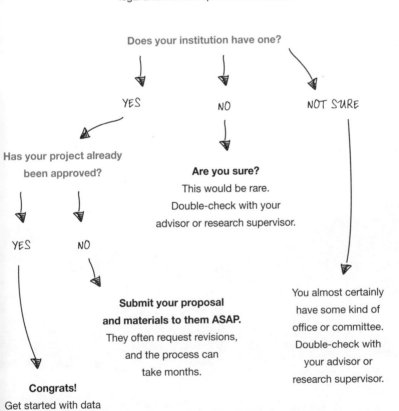

Does your institution have one?

YES   NO   NOT SURE

**Has your project already
been approved?**

YES   NO

Are you sure?
This would be rare.
Double-check with your
advisor or research supervisor.

**Submit your proposal
and materials to them ASAP.**
They often request revisions,
and the process can
take months.

You almost certainly
have some kind of
office or committee.
Double-check with
your advisor or
research supervisor.

Congrats!
Get started with data
collection ASAP.

I NOW UNDERSTAND
THE ETHICAL
CONSIDERATIONS
OF SAMPLING.

Random error and systematic,
consistent biases in sampling

How can I reduce error and bias in sampling?

summary

Selecting a bigger sample will
reduce unsystematic error;
reducing systematic bias will
require thoughtful planning.

summary

Nobody's perfect

No sample is perfectly precise. Error is simply the gap between your sample's value and the true population value. Despite your most fastidious efforts, your sample's estimates won't match the population values exactly.

Error is inevitable, but we can design and conduct projects in ways that minimize it. Sampling variance – unsystematic error due to the random luck of the draw – can be reduced by selecting a larger sample. But bias – systematic error that causes your sample to consistently stray from the population – is more complex. Two major sources of bias – flawed sampling frames that omit part of the population and participant non-response – deserve careful attention when planning your project and evaluating its findings.

SAMPLING ERROR

Error is simply the disparity between your sample's estimate – '52% of people supported the policy' – and the true population value, which is unknown. We can split error into two parts: sampling variance and sampling bias.

Sampling variance is the 'luck of the draw' inherent in random methods. If you repeatedly randomly sample from a population, you'll get different estimates of your population values each time. Sampling variance is unsystematic – the odds of your estimate being too high or too low are the same, so it doesn't tug in one direction.

The best way to reduce sampling variability is to select a larger sample. For all sampling designs, a handful of quirky cases will have less influence in a bigger sample.

Stratifying is another tool for reducing sampling variability. Creating strata won't help as much as recruiting more people, but it will prevent your sample from straying from the population on the stratifying variable.

BIAS

Bias is systematic error that consistently tugs your sample estimates away from the real population values. Bias captures all the non-random aspects of your project that result in a misleading estimate of the population. Unlike sampling variance, bias is systematic.

Like samples, dart throwers can have systematic, consistent biases. The many flaws in people's vision and technique, taken together, cause their darts to stray in one direction – too high, perhaps, or too leftward. Bias is like a consistent stray in darts. Research flaws large and small, taken together, can cause a systematic drift. Your sample's means and percentages will consistently overshoot or undershoot the bull's eye – the true population values.

BIAS FROM SAMPLING FRAMES

Flawed sampling frames are a huge source of bias. If your list that defines your population is flawed, then your sample will systematically stray. Some flaws in a sampling frame, such as duplicates, can be detected during a study and fixed later. The flaw of overcoverage – when your frame includes people who aren't in the population – can usually be handled by confirming eligibility during the survey.

The most troubling flaw is undercoverage – when the sampling frame is missing population members. Sometimes, you have a good sense of who is missing. If a professional society updates its membership list annually, you know that the list will miss new members who joined since the last update. The omitted members are probably younger and less experienced than the included ones.

But the omitted members are often an 'unknown unknown'. They might differ in some key way – age, education, political attitudes, social mobility, affluence, or wariness – that will bias your estimates. Because you rarely know if and how the missing members differ, the biasing effects of undercoverage are complex and vexing.

BIAS FROM
ON-RESPONSE

Not everyone who you select for your sample will end up providing data.
Non-response, a grave issue in sampling, has three flavours:

1 **You can't contact the person.** The rise of junk mail, spam, and
   robocalls has made contacting members vastly harder.

2 **You can't communicate,** often because of different language
   competencies.

3 **The person declines to participate,** usually without telling you
   why.

**Non-response causes bias when the non-responders differ from
the rest of the population.** The people in the population who are easier
to contact, share your language, and want to take part probably differ
from the rest in important ways. If your non-responders have attitudes
that are relatively more controversial, for example, your sample value
will stray from the population.

Researchers have developed many tools for reducing non-response:

- Contacting via many channels.

- Re-contacting non-responders and sending reminders.

- Offering incentives.

- Creating streamlined, low-friction surveys.

- Conveying credibility and professionalism.

- Explaining why the research matters.

REDUCING NON-RESPONSE

CHECKPOINT

What would non-response look like in your project?

Can't contact. Think about how you will contact people – phone calls, emails, in-person visits, and so on. What are some reasons why you wouldn't be able to reach some people?

....

....

....

....

Can't communicate. What languages do you expect your sample to speak fluently?

....

....

....

....

Person declines. What are some reasons why people would decline to take part that are specific to you and your project? What are some reasons that are general to all research?

....

....

....

....

Now list three things you can do to reduce non-response.

1 ....

2 ....

3 ....

Large samples reduce your margin of error and increase statistical power

Section

8

How large should my sample be?

summary

As large as possible – big samples
increase your project's credibility,
precision, and statistical power.

summary

How many participants do I need?

'What sample size do I need?' might be the most common question in statistics. Larger samples have two statistical virtues – your estimates have a smaller margin of error, and you have higher statistical power for significance testing. Larger samples are thus naturally more credible and persuasive to your work's audience.

The ideal sample is always large, but big samples aren't a cure-all for biases – adding more members to a small, biased sample simply yields a bigger, biased sample. And because larger samples require more time and money to collect and prepare for analysis, researchers must reconcile the ideal sample size with what is feasible.

SELECTING A SAMPLE SIZE

When it comes to sample sizes, bigger is always better:

- Increasing your sample size reduces sampling variance. As a result, larger samples have a smaller margin of error – the estimates are more precise and more likely to replicate.

- If your project uses significance testing, larger samples give you more statistical power.

- Your audience is better persuaded by large-sample studies, and for good reasons.

But because you aren't made of time and money, you must strike a balance – you need a sample size that is large enough to answer your research question but feasible given your resources and timeline.

SHRINKING YOUR MARGIN OF ERROR

Bigger samples have less sampling variance, so your sample estimates are more precise. Your project's means and percentages – such as average voter apathy and the percentage who support a political policy – are more likely to be closer to the true population values. Stated differently, your margin of error – the gap between your estimate and the true number – is smaller.

Estimating the standard error for a mean illustrates how larger samples increase precision. The standard error formula is simple:

$$SE = SD \div \sqrt{n}$$

You divide the sample's standard deviation by the square root of your sample size.

The formula shows two things:

- Your standard error always declines as your sample size goes up, all else equal.

- But the biggest declines come early: going from 100 to 200 reduces your margin of error much more than going from 1000 to 1100.

BOOSTING STATISTICAL POWER

If your project involves inferential tests – the world of p-values, null hypotheses, and statistical significance – larger samples increase your statistical power. Power is acceptable if you have at least an 80% chance of finding a significant effect (at a two-tailed, .05 alpha level) and quite good if you have a 90% chance. If you don't know how small or big your effect size will be, just compute power for a range of sizes, from much smaller to much larger than you expect.

For example, how many people would you need to test the significance of correlations? **Pearson r coefficients** are effect sizes: values of $r = .10$ (small), $r = .30$ (medium), and $r = .50$ (large) are common in power analysis. Based on G*Power, a free power-analysis program, the table displays the sample size you would need for a range of effect sizes and power levels.

Effect Size	Power = 80%	Power = 90%
$r = .10$	782	1046
$r = .20$	193	258
$r = .30$	84	112
$r = .40$	46	61
$r = .50$	29	37
$r = .60$	19	24

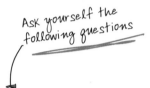

Ask yourself the
following questions

- Using software or power tables, how many people will you need for
  your expected effect size? Keep in mind that social science effect
  sizes tend to be modest, at around $r = .15$ to $r = .25$.

- Next, based on how much time you have available, how many people
  will you need to recruit per month?

- Is your sample size realistic?

GETTING MORE FROM YOUR SAMPLE

When you can't recruit more people, you can get more out of the sample size you have.

- Reduce non-response. Survey research offers many practical ideas for reducing the number of people who decline.

- Reduce other sources of error by using high-quality assessments, training the research personnel thoroughly, conducting pilot testing, and avoiding mistakes in data entry, coding, and handling.

SAMPLE SIZE ISN'T SORCERY

Size isn't a magical cure for poor sampling. A huge sample size cannot turn a snowball sample into a stratified random sample or a shabby sampling frame into a comprehensive one. Doubling your sample won't compensate for bias – you'll simply have a biased sample that is twice as big.

Work through this checklist to help ensure you have mastered all you need to know to select a sample

☐ Can you explain why researchers sample from populations? If not, see page 11.

☐ Can you define your project's population? If not, see page 23.

☐ Can you describe how probability sampling works? If not, see page 41.

☐ Can you describe the pros and cons of subjective, non-probability sampling? If not, see page 55.

HOW TO KNOW YOU ARE DONE

Do you know a way to sample from obscure and wary populations? If not, see page 71.

Have you thought through the ethical issues in identifying and contacting members of your population? If not, see page 83.

Can you describe the likely sources of error and bias and how to minimize them? If not, see page 97.

Do you have an estimate of how many people you will need? If not, see page 111.

Glossary

Bias Systematic error that causes a sample's values to differ consistently from the population values.

Census The study of an entire population, not a subset of it.

Convenience sampling A kind of non-probability sampling that recruits easy-to-find, 'at hand' samples or that has participants self-select into the project.

Elements The individual parts that make up a population, also known as members or units.

Non-probability sampling A group of methods that introduce subjective judgment into the selection of population members.

Population The larger collective that you want to understand and make claims about.

Probability sampling The gold standard for sampling, these methods randomly select elements to yield a small-scale model of the population.

Purposive sampling A non-probability sampling approach in which expert judgment is used to select at least some elements.

Quota sampling A non-probability method in which researchers set sample-size goals for different groups and recruit until each goal is met.

Sample A collection of elements selected from a larger population.

Sampling frame The 'list' of the population members that, for the practical purposes of a project, defines the population.

Sampling variance Random, unsystematic error introduced by the vagaries of chance.

Snowball sampling A non-probability method in which participants identify other population members.